I Am She

I Am She

POSITIVE & EMPOWERING AFFIRMATIONS FOR WOMEN TO AWAKEN AND CELEBRATE THE DIVINE FEMININE AND SACRED HERITAGE OF THE GODDESS WITHIN

SHANNON MACDONALD

Copyright © 2022 by Shannon MacDonald

Publication Date: 4/2022 (HC) 5/2022 (PB Ebook)

ISBN:

HC - 978-1-7365102-7-8

PB - 978-1-7365102-8-5

Ebook - 979-8-9862369-0-2

All rights reserved.

No part of this book may be reproduced in any form or by any electronic or mechanical means, including information storage and retrieval systems, without written permission from the author, except for the use of brief quotations in a book review.

The publisher and the author make no guarantees concerning the level of success you may experience by following the suggestions
and strategies contained in this book, and you accept the risk that results will differ for each individual. The information provided in this book are views and opinions of the author and is not medical, psychological, financial, religious, or political advice. This book is not intended to replace qualified professional care, services, or instruction, and does not represent or guarantee that you will achieve the same or similar results. The intent of this book is only to offer information of a general nature to help your quest for improving your life. In the event you use information in this book for yourself, the author and publisher assume no responsibility for your actions.

Dedication

For all women who are ready to remember the truth of who they are and claim their Goddess Nature and Divine Destiny.

I Am She

The Radiant Expression
of All I See.
The Dreams of Divinity
are a Reflection of Me.

Contents

A Love Letter from the Author — xiii

1. I Am She — 1
   Mother, maiden, and crone throughout infinite dreams and timeless eternity

2. I Am She — 3
   Radiating the loving presence of Awakened Awareness with my sisters in mind, body, and soul

3. I Am She — 5
   Who flows through the boundless passages of Life and Creation

4. I Am She — 7
   Healer of hearts and carrier of The Light

5. I Am She — 9
   Maiden of the moon, goddess of the stars, and womb of Life and Creation

6. I Am She — 11
   Protector and lover of all things born and yet to be born

7. I Am She — 13
   Who walks the path of the priestess as a sacred sister of ancient wisdom and divine truth

8. I Am She — 15
   Deliciously delicate, fiercely courageous, and radiantly beautiful

9. I Am She — 17
   Who illuminates the radiance of Enlightened Awareness and Divine Splendor

10. I Am She — 19
    Speaker of Truth, bearer of Love, and embodiment of The Light

11. I Am She   21
A refuge for the lost, hopeless, and helpless hearts of humanity

12. I Am She   23
Ageless Goddess and timeless temple of All Creation

13. I Am She   25
Dancing within the song of ecstatic passion and sensual love

14. I Am She   27
Who needs no excuses for her past choices, fearless actions, and warrior goddess spirit

15. I Am She   29
A fearless force of courage and unrelenting face of freedom.

16. I Am She   31
The uncompromising warrior for righteousness and defender of justice

17. I Am She   33
The womb that embodies new life for dreams to be born

18. I Am She   35
The seer of all things real and knower of all things true

19. I Am She   37
Divinity in motion and Creation in form

20. I Am She   39
The voice of courage for those who cannot speak

21. I Am She   41
The eyes of truth for those who are blind

22. I Am She   43
A sanctuary of justice for those who have been wronged

23. I Am She   45
The embrace of compassion for those who have lost their way

24. I Am She — 47
The radiance of remembrance for those who have forgotten

25. I Am She — 49
The unifying heart for humanity to heal

26. I Am She — 51
The dreamer and the dream and everything in-between

27. I Am She — 53
The Goddess of eternal love, divine forgiveness and infinite compassion

28. I Am She — 55
Claimer of my convictions and unfollower of fear

29. I Am She — 57
Eternal beauty, endless compassion, infinite wisdom and divine grace

30. I Am She — 59
The wisdom, word, and wand of The Goddess

31. I Am She — 61
The pure potential of creative imagination and divine possibilities

32. I Am She — 63
Dispeller of illusion and alchemist for divine living

33. I Am She — 65
The illuminating star of inspiration and hope for humanity

34. I Am She — 67
Who has the courage to move forward and the inner strength to continue

35. I Am She — 69
A new beginning each day and peaceful resolution each night

36. I Am She — 71
The author of my personal story of life

37. I Am She — 73
Who sees the truth of reality and radiates the vision so others may find their way

38. I Am She 75
The grace of The Goddess and the true love of The Divine

39. I Am She 77
The balance and beauty between darkness and Light

40. I Am She 79
Who opens the portals of Universal Healing and Divine Forgiveness

41. I Am She 81
Creator of nourishing thoughts and empowering beliefs that seed the world with reality

42. I Am She 83
The unifying presence and pure potential of Divine Consciousness

43. I Am She 85
The Divine Memory of Universal Awakening

44. I Am She 87
The dream seed of the ancestors and the heritage of humanity

45. I Am She 89
The wisdom and grace of the One True Name

46. I Am She 91
Inspired thoughts of Divine Imagination and actualized outcomes of the Word

47. I Am She 93
The completion of the Breath of Life as It gently inhales the next moment of creation

48. I Am She 95
Who holds the space for answered prayers and highest healing

49. I Am She 97
The face of Grace and the body of The Divine

50. I Am She 99
A self-reliant sanctuary of radiant love and infinite strength

51. I Am She 101
Who honors her voice and speaks her truth

52. I Am She 103
    A channel for infinite abundance to gracefully and easily flow through me

53. I Am She 105
    The Divine essence of all that is eternal and unchanging

54. I Am She 107
    All that I see and know myself to be. All that I feel and remember is real

About the Author 111
A Message from Shannon 115
Also by Shannon MacDonald 117

A Love Letter from the Author

Dear Divine Woman,

Throughout the ages, women have carried the seeds of Life as they embody the womb of Creation. We are all sisters within the eternal flame of Divinity. Each of us, cosmic carriers of The Light, our true essence of beauty, love, unity, and truth radiates throughout our reality because of who we are. We are the Maidens, Mothers, and Crones of the Divine Feminine.

As we awaken from the deep sleep of forgetfulness, we begin to remember the truth of our origins and our value and contribution for universal healing and enlightenment. We are united in a common cause as we rediscover our Goddess nature and Divine Feminine heritage.

As we gather in our remembrance, we unite in our love. We stand strong in our power. We are convicted in our courage as we claim the wisdom of our ancestors and reunite within our truth. From Maidens, Mothers to Crones and everything in-between, we radiate the light and love of Unity Consciousness.

I invite you now to reconnect and reclaim your Divine Feminine power and potential through the portal of your Higher Knowing. Your thoughts, beliefs, words, feelings, and actions will lead the way to that of which you dream.

As our dreams shape our reality with the vibrancy of our awakened awareness, we find ourselves looking beyond what we think we see and once thought we knew. We begin to break free from the programs of limiting beliefs, destructive illusions, and scornful division and remember the truth of who we are. YES, my dear soul sister, YOU are the love, light, beauty, and truth of The Goddess. As you claim your true heritage, you will rise within your awareness.

You hold a special place in the Order of Awakening. The more you remember, the more humanity will collectively awaken from the dream of forgetfulness as we rise to a New Earth. One that is liberated from the false realities of limiting beliefs and fear-based programs. Where we collectively remember the divine flow of Oneness within all things as we honor the holiness of life. This is the reality you have always known existed but may not have claimed. A reality where you realize you are enough and have always been enough as you remember your purpose and flow within your highest potentials. This, my divine radiant woman, are the seeds of Life and the womb of Creation *you* hold within.

The affirmations in this book are love messages that were gifted to me through my channeled transmissions from Divinity. Each message is a gateway to help open your remembrance and align your awareness with higher realms of reality. Read them slowly as you savor the life-force energy each message vibrationally represents. As you linger on the messages, allow yourself to flow within the feelings they invoke. This book is imbued with Divine Codes of Consciousness to help you gracefully awaken your awareness so that you may remember the love, light, beauty, and truth of who you are. As you flow within the heart-opening presence of your grace, you will remember.

The unifying, harmonizing, and peaceful presence of a New Earth is calling. As we awaken, we remember how to recognize and access the beauty and truth of our cosmic heritage of Life and Creation within the Light of Divinity.

Set aside your worries of worthiness, fears of the future, and disbelief of your true and radiant Divine Feminine nature. You carry the seeds of our heritage and the wisdom of the ages within your essence. You are the promise in which the hopes and dreams of our ancestors are realized as Life continues forward.

As we collectively unite in our hearts, we remember together. We light the way for others to remember their truth during this time of universal Awakening. As we gather in our love, we rise above the programs of fear and limitation. We are the Maidens, Mothers, and Crones of ageless wisdom, timeless eternity, and infinite grace.

The dearest thing you can imagine to be is the life you most desire to see. See your life with confidence and grace; you are whole, complete, happy, healthy, and safe.

Always remember... you are She!

With great love, divine remembrance, and soulful awakening,

Shannon MacDonald

ONE
I Am She

**MOTHER, MAIDEN, AND CRONE THROUGHOUT
INFINITE DREAMS AND TIMELESS ETERNITY**

I dream the collective dreams of triumph for all women throughout all time. I hold the remembrance of oneness and wisdom of The Goddess within my soul.

TWO
I Am She

RADIATING THE LOVING PRESENCE OF
AWAKENED AWARENESS WITH MY SISTERS IN
MIND, BODY, AND SOUL

My radiance illuminates the world with compassion, peace, unity, and grace. I am the face of all women and the heart of The Divine.

THREE
I Am She

**WHO FLOWS THROUGH THE BOUNDLESS
PASSAGES OF LIFE AND CREATION**

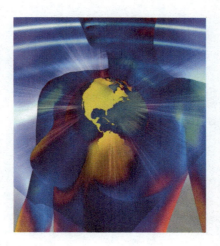

I merge with the Divine Mother within every moment of stillness. The river of eternal truth flows through me and all my sisters in body and spirit as we meet in the silent solitude of our hearts.

FOUR
I Am She

HEALER OF HEARTS AND CARRIER OF THE LIGHT

Divine Light illuminates my way through all stages of my life. As I radiate The Light, I unify and heal the hearts of humanity. I honor my radiance and trust my Higher Knowing.

FIVE
I Am She

**MAIDEN OF THE MOON, GODDESS OF
THE STARS, AND WOMB OF LIFE AND CREATION**

I am the body and spirit of The Divine Mother. I flow throughout timeless eternity with grace and ease. I birth new beginnings with every thought, feeling, belief, and word.

SIX
I Am She

**PROTECTOR AND LOVER OF ALL THINGS BORN
AND YET TO BE BORN**

I am a fierce warrior of The Light as I defend and protect the sacred sanctity of life. To honor me is to honor all life and creation.

SEVEN
I Am She

WHO WALKS THE PATH OF THE PRIESTESS AS A SACRED SISTER OF ANCIENT WISDOM AND DIVINE TRUTH

I honor the wisdom of the ages and carry the echoes of the ancestors within my heart.

EIGHT
I Am She

**DELICIOUSLY DELICATE,
FIERCELY COURAGEOUS, AND RADIANTLY
BEAUTIFUL**

I celebrate my beauty, rejoice in my divine feminine nature, and honor my warrior Goddess Spirit. I remember my strength and call upon my courage to protect truth and defend righteousness.

NINE
I Am She

WHO ILLUMINATES THE RADIANCE OF ENLIGHTENED AWARENESS AND DIVINE SPLENDOR

My light is the Light of eternal truth and Divine Illumination. I am all that I see. The dreams of Divinity are an expression of me.

TEN
I Am She

SPEAKER OF TRUTH, BEARER OF LOVE, AND EMBODIMENT OF THE LIGHT

My heart illuminates my mind to see the truth. My words are spoken to reflect what I know inside, not what I see outside. If I need clarity on any topic, I remember my true nature of Light and ask to be enlightened within the silence of my heart.

ELEVEN

I Am She

A REFUGE FOR THE LOST, HOPELESS, AND HELPLESS HEARTS OF HUMANITY

I am the embodiment of The Divine. I represent the Light that illuminates all darkness and dispels all fear. There is no illusion or false reality that can diminish my truth or weaken my Light.

TWELVE
I Am She

AGELESS GODDESS AND TIMELESS TEMPLE OF ALL CREATION

My beauty reflects the nature of reality and the essence of The Goddess. I am the timeless face of Divine Radiance, eternal love, beauty, and grace.

THIRTEEN
I Am She

DANCING WITHIN THE SONG OF ECSTATIC
PASSION AND SENSUAL LOVE

My heart beats to the Universal Song of Life and Creation. As the music plays from the orchestra of The Divine, I dance to the rhythm of my One True Love. I honor my sensual nature and celebrate my divine pleasures.

FOURTEEN
I Am She

WHO NEEDS NO EXCUSES FOR HER PAST CHOICES, FEARLESS ACTIONS, AND WARRIOR GODDESS SPIRIT

Where I am right now is where I am supposed to be. I respectfully reflect on my choices and learn from my experiences. I move with clarity, courage, and grace to the next chapter of my life. I look back on my life in gratitude for the lessons I learned.

FIFTEEN
I Am She

**A FEARLESS FORCE OF COURAGE AND
UNRELENTING FACE OF FREEDOM.**

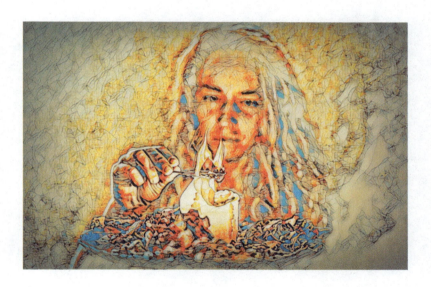

My mistakes are mine and no one else's. They were necessary for my life to bring me to who I am today. I am a survivor of personal wars within, a believer of my strength and power, and a receiver of Divine forgiveness for my past transgressions.

SIXTEEN
I Am She

THE UNCOMPROMISING WARRIOR FOR RIGHTEOUSNESS AND DEFENDER OF JUSTICE

I fight for the rights of the victims of oppression and uphold the laws of Universal Truth. I allow myself to look beyond limiting beliefs so I may represent The Goddess in my highest capacity.

SEVENTEEN
I Am She

THE WOMB THAT EMBODIES NEW LIFE FOR DREAMS TO BE BORN

I am the temple for the divine dream of The Goddess. As dreams flow through me, the experience of Life unfolds. I embrace the dreams of Creation and celebrate the birth of new realities.

EIGHTEEN
I Am She

THE SEER OF ALL THINGS REAL AND KNOWER OF ALL THINGS TRUE

I am The Divine Mother of life and creation. I see the truth of reality when my mind is in tune with my heart. In my natural state of awareness, the path to truth becomes clear.

NINETEEN
I Am She

DIVINITY IN MOTION AND CREATION IN FORM

I am the voice in which I sing and the song in which I dream. As I move my body through the world of form, I honor my true self, celebrate my divine feminine nature, and revel in the ecstatic dance of life.

TWENTY
I Am She

THE VOICE OF COURAGE FOR THOSE WHO CANNOT SPEAK

As I listen to The Divine Within, I remember my truth and step into my power. I channel the voice of The Goddess. I speak for the ones who are lost, alone, and afraid and cannot speak for themselves. My voice is their voice. My courage is their courage.

TWENTY-ONE

I Am She

THE EYES OF TRUTH FOR THOSE WHO ARE BLIND

For every soul who remains in the darkness of fear or the shadows of illusion, I offer my inner vision and perfect sight of Divinity, to see the truth of awakening and the beauty of Reality.

TWENTY-TWO
I Am She

A SANCTUARY OF JUSTICE FOR THOSE WHO HAVE BEEN WRONGED

As I expand into my Higher Knowing, I see my mission to be of service. I radiate the love and light of Divinity within me so I may be a refuge for the helpless, hopeless, and hurting hearts of humanity.

TWENTY-THREE
I Am She

**THE EMBRACE OF COMPASSION FOR THOSE
WHO HAVE LOST THEIR WAY**

As I awaken my awareness I see the fears of the ones who are still asleep. I open my heart and expand my Light to help them find their way.

TWENTY-FOUR
I Am She

THE RADIANCE OF REMEMBRANCE FOR THOSE WHO HAVE FORGOTTEN

As I look beyond what I think I see, I remember the hidden history of truth behind the illusions of fear. The Great Remembrance rises within the universal awakening of humanity.

TWENTY-FIVE
I Am She

THE UNIFYING HEART FOR HUMANITY TO HEAL

I am a living temple of divine transformation. My body holds the energetic Codes of Awakening to help unify and heal the hearts of humanity as we rise to a New Earth together.

TWENTY-SIX
I Am She

THE DREAMER AND THE DREAM AND EVERYTHING IN-BETWEEN

I am the actualized experience of the One Divine Dream. As I look beyond what I think I see, I become who I dream myself to be.

TWENTY-SEVEN
I Am She

THE GODDESS OF ETERNAL LOVE, DIVINE FORGIVENESS AND INFINITE COMPASSION

I look through the eyes of love and the heart of forgiveness for all things. I forgive my transgressions, I let go of regret, and I forgive the wrongdoings of others. I allow myself to be released from suffering.

TWENTY-EIGHT
I Am She

CLAIMER OF MY CONVICTIONS AND
UNFOLLOWER OF FEAR

I see through the illusions of a fear-based reality when I remember to place my attention on truth and love. I see the difference between truth and illusion as I guide my awareness away from fear.

TWENTY-NINE
I Am She

**ETERNAL BEAUTY, ENDLESS COMPASSION,
INFINITE WISDOM AND DIVINE GRACE**

I am all I believe myself to be. I love myself and believe in my worthiness. I am glorious, smart, beautiful, strong, joyful, independent, and courageous. I am Divinely guided and supported.

THIRTY
I Am She

THE WISDOM, WORD, AND WAND OF THE GODDESS

I am the actualized experience of The Goddess. I am the embodiment of Divinity. My thoughts, words, feelings, and beliefs hold the vibration of Infinite Creation.

THIRTY-ONE
I Am She

THE PURE POTENTIAL OF CREATIVE IMAGINATION AND DIVINE POSSIBILITIES

I am the universal dream of Divine Inspiration for all women and the canvas in which She creates Her masterpiece of life.

THIRTY-TWO
I Am She

DISPELLER OF ILLUSION AND ALCHEMIST FOR DIVINE LIVING

I cut the cords of fear, illusion, limitation, and disempowering habits as I remember my Goddess within. I radiate the truth, the light, and the way towards enlightened living.

THIRTY-THREE
I Am She

THE ILLUMINATING STAR OF INSPIRATION AND HOPE FOR HUMANITY

The radiance of my love and the luminosity of my Light is a portal for Cosmic Consciousness to awaken, truth to be known, and hope to be restored.

THIRTY-FOUR
I Am She

WHO HAS THE COURAGE TO MOVE FORWARD AND THE INNER STRENGTH TO CONTINUE

I am empowered by the Light of my Higher Awareness. She guides me to the destiny of my dreams. I listen to Her voice in the stillness of my heart and build my confidence through Her clarity.

THIRTY-FIVE
I Am She

A NEW BEGINNING EACH DAY AND PEACEFUL RESOLUTION EACH NIGHT

I begin each day with the remembrance of my purpose and lay my head down each night in gratitude for the opportunity to serve my Creator.

THIRTY-SIX
I Am She

THE AUTHOR OF MY PERSONAL STORY OF LIFE

My heartbreaks, sorrows, joys, and triumphs are all part of my life story. I have a new opportunity each moment to write a new chapter and heal the wounds within me. I learn from my lessons and grow from their experiences.

THIRTY-SEVEN
I Am She

WHO SEES THE TRUTH OF REALITY AND RADIATES THE VISION SO OTHERS MAY FIND THEIR WAY

I am patient with others who are still in the darkness of worldly fears and programmed realities. I remember the candle of Divine Illumination is ever-present within me. I am a beacon for truth and an emissary of The Light.

THIRTY-EIGHT
I Am She

THE GRACE OF THE GODDESS AND THE TRUE LOVE OF THE DIVINE

I remember I am enough and I have always been enough. I know that the measure of my worth is not from what others think, but who I know I am. I am pure love, radiant beauty, and Divine Light.

THIRTY-NINE
I Am She

THE BALANCE AND BEAUTY BETWEEN DARKNESS AND LIGHT

I embrace the darkness and the light in my life. All of my experiences have made me who I am today. I remember my Goddess nature of Light and bless the lessons I have learned.

FORTY

I Am She

WHO OPENS THE PORTALS OF UNIVERSAL HEALING AND DIVINE FORGIVENESS

I am my own highest healer. Every memory carries my story of love and loss, pain and pleasure. I have the ability to forgive the past and heal the wounds within me.

FORTY-ONE
I Am She

CREATOR OF NOURISHING THOUGHTS AND EMPOWERING BELIEFS THAT SEED THE WORLD WITH REALITY

My focused attention, thoughts, feelings, and words are planted in the garden of my creations. Each moment brings new opportunities to choose what I think, believe, focus on, and say.

FORTY-TWO
I Am She

THE UNIFYING PRESENCE AND PURE POTENTIAL OF DIVINE CONSCIOUSNESS

I am here to experience, create, love, and learn. All roads lead to the possibilities and potentials of Infinite Creation. Divine inspiration guides me on the path of my purpose and helps me flow within my highest potentials.

FORTY-THREE
I Am She

THE DIVINE MEMORY OF UNIVERSAL AWAKENING

When I remember my Goddess nature and look beyond the illusions of fear and distraction I remember my soul's mission to radiate The Light.

FORTY-FOUR
I Am She

THE DREAM SEED OF THE ANCESTORS AND THE HERITAGE OF HUMANITY

I am the living dream of our ancestors. I hold them respectfully in my heart and honor their visions for an enlightened world. I shine my Light each day to plant their dream seeds for awakening and restore our reality as one harmonious human race.

FORTY-FIVE
I Am She

THE WISDOM AND GRACE OF THE ONE TRUE NAME

I am the embodiment of The Divine. The one that is nameless yet is known in the hearts of all who remember. I celebrate my True Name, yet it is unknown to my ears. I honor my Creator as I eat from the table of divine wisdom and drink from the cup of eternal grace.

FORTY-SIX
I Am She

INSPIRED THOUGHTS OF DIVINE IMAGINATION AND ACTUALIZED OUTCOMES OF THE WORD

I stay vigilant in seeding my thoughts with inspiration and meaning and cultivating my words with truth and compassion.

FORTY-SEVEN
I Am She

THE COMPLETION OF THE BREATH OF LIFE AS IT GENTLY INHALES THE NEXT MOMENT OF CREATION

Each morning upon waking I have a new chance to experience life. Each night I fall into the loving embrace of The Divine as the dreams of The Creator unfold within me.

FORTY-EIGHT
I Am She

**WHO HOLDS THE SPACE FOR ANSWERED
PRAYERS AND HIGHEST HEALING**

My feelings are my prayers that originate from my heart. I hold reverence for my highest feelings and know my prayers will be answered within the messages of divine inspiration and unconditional love.

FORTY-NINE
I Am She

THE FACE OF GRACE AND THE BODY OF THE DIVINE

I love my body unconditionally and am grateful for how it moves me through life. Anytime I have feelings of self-judgment or unworthiness, I remember that I am the instrument for Divinity to flow.

FIFTY
I Am She

A SELF-RELIANT SANCTUARY OF RADIANT LOVE AND INFINITE STRENGTH

I am a sovereign force within the storms of doubt, ridicule, and fear. I am an independent and capable queen of my creations. I face challenges with clarity, courage, and grace.

FIFTY-ONE
I Am She

WHO HONORS HER VOICE AND SPEAKS HER TRUTH

What I have to say is valid and important. I allow my voice to express my wants, needs, dreams, and desires. My words are my wand. They radiate truth and the power of my True Identity.

FIFTY-TWO
I Am She

A CHANNEL FOR INFINITE ABUNDANCE TO GRACEFULLY AND EASILY FLOW THROUGH ME

I have enough time, resources, inspiration, and support to follow my heart and live my dreams with higher vision, purpose, power, and passion.

FIFTY-THREE
I Am She

THE DIVINE ESSENCE OF ALL THAT IS ETERNAL AND UNCHANGING

As all things in physical form eventually come to an end, I remember my eternal nature and infinite expression of Source. I celebrate and honor all stages of life, transition, and re-birth.

FIFTY-FOUR
I Am She

ALL THAT I SEE AND KNOW MYSELF TO BE. ALL THAT I FEEL AND REMEMBER IS REAL

I am The Divine Radiant Goddess of Life and Creation, awakening my awareness, remembering my truth, and discovering my peace, power, purpose, passion, and highest potentials. There is no one to be other than me. I AM SHE!

I Am She

About the Author

Shannon MacDonald is a bestselling author, spiritual channel, healer, and ascension code activator who pioneers the realms of spiritual awakening and higher consciousness communication. Her books, services, and events serve as gateways to enlightened living, guiding individuals to transcend fear and limiting beliefs, aligning them with their inner truth, higher healing, and infinite potentials. As an Emissary of the Light and

Channel for advanced dimensional realities, Shannon leads explorations through quantum consciousness, aiding in humanity's collective awakening and ascension.

Shannon began her journey in healthcare as a registered nurse in 1992, quickly recognizing her innate calling as a healer. Beyond conventional medicine, she noticed that her patients experienced less physical and emotional pain and often healed in profound ways when she was energetically attuned to them. This realization led her to explore and master various energy healing modalities, including Reiki, Reconnective Healing, and Quantum Healing.

Today, Shannon stands at the forefront of spiritual awakening, quantum healing, and consciousness exploration. Her books, services, and events not only offer paths to personal transformation but also serve as conduits for enlightened living and conscious creation. She dedicates herself to helping individuals realize their true nature and infinite potentials, guiding them to transcend limitations often imposed by years of programmed beliefs and disempowering patterns.

Residing in Florida with her husband and their beloved German Shepherd, Shannon cherishes spending time with her loved ones, immersing herself in nature, cycling, and enjoying motorcycle rides. Her life's work supports others in reconnecting with higher awareness, elevating their vibrational frequency, and embracing their roles as conscious creators, fundamentally shifting realities for the better. Shannon provides unparalleled guidance and support for those on a quest for a more purposeful and impactful existence.

Visit Shannon online to learn more:
ShannonMacDonald.net

A Message from Shannon

HELP SPREAD THE WORD ABOUT MY BOOKS

If you enjoyed this book and feel like it gave you some value, I would appreciate a **review on Amazon.** I am a self-published author and don't have a marketing team behind me. What I have is YOU!

FOLLOW ME!

Follow Me on **You Tube** for inspirational messages, guided meditations and topics on awakening.

youtube.com/@ShannonMacDonaldAuthor

Follow me on **Medium** for transformational articles to support your awakened awareness.

medium.com/@ShannonMacDonaldAuthor

LETS CONNECT

Sign up for my **mailing list** and become a part of my spiritual family.

ShannonMacDonald.net/sign-up

Thank you! Your support means a lot to me.

Also by Shannon MacDonald

New Earth Reality
The Other Side of Ascension
The Great Liberation

Sequel to New Earth Rising

As humanity approaches The Great Liberation and Ascension to the New Earth, *The Other Side of Ascension* continues with vital questions for humanity to consider and new information to absorb regarding The Great Liberation of human consciousness and the next sitting of Reality.

ShannonMacDonald.net/the-other-side-of-ascension-book

New Earth Rising
Starseed Transmissions for Awakening, Activation, and Ascension

Channeled messages revealing Earth's hidden history, cosmic origins, and the true nature of Reality and Ascension.

Awaken higher awareness, activate dormant consciousness and liberate from false reality programs that steal our free will and hijack our conscious evolution.

ShannonMacDonald.net/new-earth-rising-book

Breaking Free

*Unfollow the Fear, Unplug from the Programs,
Unsubscribe from the Propaganda*

Learn How to discern TRUTH in information, facts over fallacy, and find freedom from fear. A book for Awakened Living.

Discover how you can liberate your mind and have clear access to paradigm-shifting ideas and life-transforming truth about reality.

ShannonMacDonald.net/breaking-free-book

Mastering Manifestation

*12 Keys to Unlock Your Hidden Potential
and Live the Life of Your Dreams*

Are you ready to tap into your infinite potentials and re-envision your reality?

Learn how you can supercharge your magnetic qualities as a conscious creator to set you up for success in all areas of your life.

Discover the 12 Keys to living your best life regardless of what the world looks like around you.

ShannonMacDonald.net/mastering-manifestation-book

The No News Diet
Detox from Information Overload

A healthy diet doesn't just include the quantity and quality of food you put into your mouth. It also includes the ideas and information you put into your mind.

Learn how to detoxify from the effects of informational overeating and reset your energetic microbiome to a happier, healthier, more hopeful place.

ShannonMacDonald.net/the-no-news-diet-book

How to Find Inner Peace
Awaken to Your Happiness, Purpose, and Highest Potentials

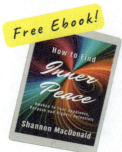

Becoming present with your Inner Peace isn't about adding another thing to your to-do list or waiting for the world to change.

Discover simple strategies how you can create your most peaceful, powerful, purposeful, and joyful life today.

ShannonMacDonald.net

Explore all of Shannon's transformational books:

ShannonMacDonald.net

Made in the USA
Monee, IL
25 November 2024

71118612R00079